Finding Out About
LIFE IN BRITAIN
IN THE 1930s

Cherry Gilchrist

Batsford Academic and Educational   *London*

Contents

Frontispiece: A scene from the film *Stand Up and Cheer*, with Shirley Temple and James Dunn.

Typeset by Tek-Art Ltd, Kent
and printed in Spain by
Grijelmo SA, Bilbao
for the publishers
Batsford Academic and Educational,
an imprint of B. T. Batsford Ltd,
4 Fitzhardinge Street
London W1H 0AH

ISBN 0 7134 4352 9

ACKNOWLEDGMENTS

The Author and Publishers would like to thank the following for their kind permission to reproduce copyright illustrations: Beamish North of England Open Air Museum, pages 9, 10; BBC Hulton Picture Library, pages 6-7, 13, 14, 15, 29, 43 (top); the Commissioner of Police of the Metropolis, page 28; Mr Michael Deering, pages 16, 22, 43; House of Fraser, pages 25, 26; Mr Arthur Oakes, page 34; Mrs Betty Owen, page 38; Mrs Kathleen Phillips, pages 20, 40-1; *Punch*, page 33; Twentieth Century Fox, frontispiece. The map on page 47 was drawn by Rudolph Britto.

Introduction

During the late 1920s and for much of the 1930s, Britain was in the grip of a financial crisis which has come to be known as "the Depression". There were not enough jobs or money to go round; in the early 1930s several million people could not find work, and many more were living on very low wages. Sometimes wages were cut, and workers often accepted this rather than risk losing their jobs altogether.

There was a big difference between the rich and the poor at this time. At one end of the scale, the wealthy could afford to keep servants, to run a house both in London and in the country, to travel on luxury holidays abroad and to shop in high-class stores. At the other, a family of eight or more people might be living in only two or three rooms, with no running water in the building, no proper furniture and no inside lavatory. Their living space was often infested with bugs, rats and mice.

1931 was a year of crisis, when the Labour Government in power found that it could not cope with the economic problems. Ramsay Macdonald, the Prime Minister, agreed to form a National Government, in which some members of the Labour, Conservative and Liberal parties all joined together in office. National Government lasted until 1939, when war broke out. After an election later in 1931, the balance of the Government became strongly Conservative, and it was "middle-of-the-road" in its policies. Some historians say that this resulted in a more stable period for Britain than for many other countries in Europe, where governments tended to be extreme in their right or left wing views.

The National Government was criticized for doing too little to give immediate help to the poorer people in Britain. However, in the longer term, it did succeed in bringing about an economic improvement. From 1933 the country began to recover from the Depression, and wages gradually rose, although it took several years longer for the worst effects of poverty to be relieved. Major industries had been particularly badly hit, since key products such as coal, steel, iron and cotton could not be sold in such large quantities either at home or abroad. Thus it was in the areas where these industries had been especially important that unemployment was worst, such as in the North of England and in parts of Wales.

The National Government was not able to help all these industries recover completely, but it was able to improve the economy both through a better financial policy and through investing money in the "rearmament" programme from about 1936 onwards. This involved manufacturing equipment such as guns, aeroplanes and ammunition which would be needed if Britain went to war with Germany. In view of Hitler's invasion of other countries in Europe, most people realized towards the end of the 1930s that Britain would become involved sooner or later in the struggle to try to prevent Germany taking over. The rearmament projects helped to reduce unemployment considerably.

New industries also provided more work. Some of them were set up because of the demand for the latest "consumer" goods, such as gramophones, wirelesses, ready-made clothes, ice-cream and motor cars. New artificial materials such as "Bakelite" (an early form of plastic) and rayon (a textile like silk) meant that certain items, such as ladies' underwear and kitchen utensils, could be made cheaply and sold in large quantities. More factories were built, and these could now run off electricity instead of using coal as in former times. Although electricity was not new in the 1930s, its possibilities were only now really being explored. Electrically-run factories were cleaner, and could be built in places where there had been no major industry before, such as on the outskirts of cities and in towns where there were no coalfields nearby.

In 1935, the National Electricity Grid had been completed, which meant that most private homes could have an electricity supply connected. This did away with the need for oil-filled lamps and for large supplies of dusty coal to keep the house warm. In housing there was a general drive towards a cleaner and more streamlined way of life. The realization that dreadful slums existed intensified the desire to clear away the musty remains of the Victorian age. Many old buildings were knocked down and replaced with less ornate, more functional ones. Home fittings and furniture of the period were designed to be easy to clean; too many ornaments and pictures in a room were frowned upon, as it was thought they would attract dust and germs. The fashion was to dislike anything floral or fussy, and to go instead for angular or geometric patterns, with zig-zags, stripes, lightning flashes and other "jazz" or "modernistic" motifs. Light colours, such as cream and pale green, were preferred for walls, and for textiles and furniture, strong, clean colours such as black and orange or else neutral shades such as beige. Of course, many people still used older furnishings and lived in Victorian or Edwardian-style houses, but the fashions described here are what we now think of as "typical" of the 1930s period, and reflect what you would find in advertisements and shopping displays of the time.

The 1920s had been a lively decade, with outrageous fashions. The 1930s was a quieter era, and there was more emphasis on dressing and behaving in a respectable manner. Because there was so much uncertainty about jobs and money, many people preferred to live a quiet and stable life rather than to look for excitement. They found a certain amount of glamour in the entertainment provided by the cinema and the radio, but their chief efforts went into finding and keeping a good job to try to keep themselves and their families from facing hardship.

=Useful Sources=

1. PEOPLE

Fortunately, there are many people who can recall what life was like in the 1930s, and you are sure to find someone among your relatives and neighbours who can talk to you about those days. You will find it helpful if you are able to make a tape recording of the conversation.

The librarian at your local library may be able to show you, or tell you where to find, old maps, photos, postcards, newspaper cuttings, etc, which relate to your town or village as it was in the 1930s. From these, you may learn about local events and about any house- or road-building that went on during the period.

2. BUILDINGS

There are many 1930s buildings in the towns and suburbs, and with a little practice you will soon be able to recognize them from their style. Look especially for estates of 1930s detached and semi-detached houses, and for cinemas and factories. Cinemas are often used for other purposes now, such as social clubs and Bingo Halls, but you can sometimes still see the old name – for example, Regal or Odeon – on the front of the building. The factories were often built close to by-passes or ring roads, on the outskirts of a town.

3. VISUAL MATERIAL

a) *Photos* Family albums may yield a few snap shots from the 1930s. Your nearest large town is likely to have a photographic section in its local history archive which is often attached to the public library, town museum or county records office. However, the photos are not always well-classified and you will probably need to ask the person in charge for assistance. Your local newspaper may have a photo collection going back that far; check to see if it can be looked at by the public.

b) *Objects* Many items from the 1930s are still in general use, or are sold as "antiques" in shops. You can have great fun looking around junk shops and antique markets for clothes, ornaments and household objects of the period. For pictures of town and country views, events, royalty, film and sports stars, fashions and so on, try looking for

Stamps are another useful source. Can you identify the ▷
portraits on these?

cigarette cards and postcards of the period, which are relatively easy to find and often cheap to buy.

Some museums contain a selection of objects and photos from the 1930s. Local museums, folk, industrial and farming museums are particularly good in this respect.

4. WRITTEN SOURCES

a) *Books – Non-Fiction* Try the history section of your library, and also sections dealing with individual topics such as farming, costume, etc. You will often find a chapter or two dealing with the 1930s and may be lucky enough to find a book that deals solely with this period.

b) *Fiction* Look for stories written in the 1930s (check the date of the first publication which should be just inside the front of the book). They will often give you interesting details about the way of life of the period.

c) *Autobiography* Accounts which people have written of their own lives can be an excellent source of information. The librarian may be able to help you find some which relate to the 1930s. What autobiographies have been used for quotations in this book?

d) *Directories and Guides* In a reference library you can often find 1930s editions of *Kelly's Directories* for different towns, listing the inhabitants, businesses and so on. (You will find an example in the *Shopping* section, pages 26-27.) There may also be guide books produced in the 1930s.

e) *Documents and Records* All the speeches made in Parliament are recorded in *Hansard,* and most major reference libraries will have copies of this. It is not always easy reading, but can be helpful if you want to look up a particular debate. The volumes are indexed so that you can check if speeches were made on a particular subject – the Means Test, for example.

f) *School log books* and *Council Minutes* are often deposited at the town or county records office or sometimes in large public libraries. These archives also keep many private documents and family records, some of which will relate to the 1930s. A book called *Record Repositories in Great Britain*

(HMSO) will help you locate your nearest office if necessary, and you should be able to find this book in your local reference library. If you wish to visit the records office, it is best if you can ask your teacher to make arrangements in advance for a group of you to go, so that the teacher and the archivist can work out what particular material would be of most interest to you and have it ready.

g) *Magazines and Newspapers* Magazines of the period, if you can find them, give a fascinating glimpse into the life of the times. Illustrated, topical and women's magazines are among the most interesting. Enquire in your local reference library whether they have back copies of any magazines or newspapers dating from the 1930s, and also look in second-hand bookshops and at collectors' fairs. Take note of the advertisements in old magazines and newspapers, for you can learn almost as much from them as you can from articles and photographs. If you study the advertisements quoted and reproduced in this book, you will see why.

If you know of a local charity that organizes a waste paper collection, you could ask them to save you any old papers or magazines they are given from the 1930s; sometimes this happens when a house is cleared out or someone moves home.

Examples of newspapers in print in the 1930s are *The Times, The News Chronicle, The Daily Mirror.* Magazines included *Picture Post, Illustrated London News, Radio Times, Good Housekeeping, Woman's Journal, Country Life;* and for children, *The Magnet, Girl's School Friend, Hotspur, The Rainbow, Bubbles* and *The Children's Newspaper.*

Kings and Queens

KING GEORGE V AND QUEEN MARY

On 6 May 1935, George and Mary had been King and Queen for twenty-five years, and their Silver Jubilee was celebrated throughout Britain. In the evening, many bonfires were lit on hilltops as an exciting climax to the day.

> **Last night I saw half England ablaze. In an aeroplane specially chartered by the News Chronicle I took off with my pilot from Croydon aerodrome in the falling darkness of what had been a superb summer's day, in time to watch the chain of Jubilee beacons leap into flame across the country side. . . . First one, then – as if in answer – another and another, until at last the line of flaming beacons stretched away. . . . Smoke poured away in thick columns while strange little figures, like insects when their nest has been disturbed, hurried and stumbled about, this way and that, on the verge of each circle of light, limbs waving, faces glowing red in the flames.** (*News Chronicle*, 7 May 1935)

It was unusual to fly in those days, and the reporter is trying to show how different things could look from the air. Do you think he succeeds in this, and if so, how?

THE ABDICATION

After George V died in 1936, his son Edward VIII was proclaimed King. But before he was crowned, he decided to give up the throne because he wanted to marry a lady who had been divorced. Many important people in Parliament and in the Church of England thought that it would be quite wrong for him to be King if he married Mrs Simpson. The document he had to sign was called the Instrument of Abdication, and it said:

The Coronation procession in 1937. What special arrangements have been made to cope with the crowds that have gathered here?

I, Edward the Eighth, of Great Britain, Ireland, and the British Dominions beyond the Seas, King, Emperor of India, do hereby declare My irrevocable determination to renounce the Throne for Myself, and for My descendants, and My desire that effect should be given to this Instrument of Abdication immediately.

You can tell from this that the Sovereign of Great Britain ruled over a number of countries. Try to find a map in a history atlas or textbook to see which areas were British territory at the time.

THE CORONATION

In 1937, Edward's brother, George VI, was crowned King. People camped out in the streets of London to see the procession, while many of those who stayed at home organized street parties like the one in Southampton which Nancy Sharman attended. (You can find out more about Nancy Sharman on page 46.)

In Guildford Street we had a tremendous party, with everybody's kitchen tables and chairs in a long line down the middle of the road. The houses were festooned with flags and bunting and we all wore red, white and blue, even if only in the form of a ribbon. Hats were homemade and came in all shapes and sizes. Everybody going to the party took something for the tables, which were groaning with jellies, custards, fruit cakes and sandwiches. The school children brought their own blue coronation glasses, which had been presented at school. . . . We . . . danced and sang to accordions, banjoes, and even a piano which someone had got out on the pavement. . . . One little old lady did a clog dance in her husband's great boots. . . . It was indeed a grand and memorable day. The old enjoyed it as much as the young, who went to bed tired but happy. It was our own King and Queen; they belonged to us as much as we belonged to them. We were British and proud of it. Nancy Sharman, *Nothing to Steal*, Kaye and Ward, 1977)

Do you remember a Royal occasion which you celebrated? If so, you could write an account of it in the same way.

7

Poverty and Unemployment

In the early 1930s many people were out of work or living on very small earnings. In 1932, 3 million people were registered as unemployed, but it was thought that at least 10 million did not have enough money to pay for proper food and housing. When a man had no job he received some "dole" money every week from the Government, but this would only be about 32/– for a family with two children under 14, and about 15/– for a single man. Out of this it was almost impossible to pay the rent and to buy sufficient food, coal and clothing. The Government imposed the "Means Test"; they sent round inspectors to investigate people's homes, and if they thought that some of the furniture could be sold to raise money, or that a person in the family was earning even a few shillings a week, then the "dole" would be cut off and no more help given. By 1938 the number of people out of work was falling, but for most of the 1930s the problem was very severe.

STRUGGLING TO SURVIVE

Poor people found it very hard to keep up a respectable appearance, and this made it even more difficult to find a new job. Max Cohen lived in an industrial town in the north west of England, and was a skilled cabinet-maker (furniture maker) who lost his job through no fault of his own. He recorded his grim experiences of searching for work and suffering illness, depression and near starvation in *I was One of the Unemployed,* which he wrote in 1945.

> **Little things, that a person who is earning wages scarcely bothers about, have now assumed great moment and significance in your thoughts. Maybe your shoe-laces have broken and been tied together and broken again, and it is now imperative that you buy another pair. Maybe your razor-blade will no longer shave you, and it is necessary for you to buy another one. Possibly you need a haircut; but how can you afford it? Your trousers are falling to pieces, they have been patched too many times; but you don't know how you are going to get another pair. It is raining, your feet are wet, you squelch water at every step. Your shoes are cracked beyond repair, the soles are dropping off in pieces, the heels have worn down to nothing.**

"MASS OBSERVATION"

There was a growing interest in finding out about how other people lived, and writers and journalists set out to conduct what they called "Mass Observation". George Orwell was asked by the Left Book Club to visit some of the poorer areas of Lancashire and Yorkshire and to describe what he found. His book, *The Road to Wigan Pier* (1937), is an account of the miserable conditions there. He made notes of what some of the houses were like:

> **House in Peel Street. Back to back, two up, two down and large cellar. Living-room 10ft square with copper and sink. Distance to lavatory 70 yards. Four beds in house for eight people – two old parents, two adult girls ... one young man, and three children. Parents have one bed, eldest son another, and remaining five people share the other two. Bugs very bad – 'You can't keep 'em down when it's 'ot.' Indescribable squalour in downstairs room and smell upstairs almost unbearable.**

What particular problems is Orwell showing us? Look at the picture of a "slum" home and try to see what aspects of poverty are revealed in it.

June 1936

Mr S O Davies (MP for Merthyr Tydfil) – 'Are we justified in bringing this vast and brutal system of espionage into use? . . . I hate the thought of it. I hate the circumstances of these people . . . some of them first-class coal hewers, iron and steel workers. Some of them young men who have never had a day's work, but who have the will to work and a hunger for work. . . . Only this morning in coming from my home to London I had to occupy myself to see that three children under 16 should get from their homes in Merthyr Tydfil safe to Paddington Station in London – two young girls and a young boy. They were two bright and intelligent girls . . . girls who were obviously mentally suited to education. What is breaking up their home? What is driving these children out? . . . It is the wicked means test . . . compelling them to come to this city to work for a few shillings a week!'
(*Hansard Parliamentary Proceedings*)

Why is the Means Test the cause of these young people leaving home?

Some charities and government bodies tried to help those in real need, although many people preferred to go without, rather than suffer the "shame" of being given free food or clothes. Nancy Sharman and her brother and sister used to eat free meals:

At Northam, there was a meals centre for children in dire need. They came from all over Southampton and, if they lived too far out to walk, they were given a blue tram token. Breakfast was at 8.00 am and consisted of half a slice of bread and margarine and half a slice of bread and jam with a mug of cocoa. This was served on Monday, Wednesday and Friday mornings. On the other days, breakfast consisted of a bowl of very thin porridge or watery milk and a slice of bread. Dinners were more varied, with lots of potatoes and minced meat but, unfortunately for most children there was sometimes Irish stew which they hated because it was so thin and had bits of fat floating on the top. On two days a week there were apples or oranges as extras given out instead of pudding. This was the highlight of the free meals for many. I think there must have been some two hundred who attended this meals centre (Nancy Sharman, *Nothing to Steal*)

1933, North Shields, near Newcastle-upon-Tyne.

Work

STARTING WORK IN AN OFFICE

Young people were allowed to leave school at fourteen; they were encouraged to get a secure job, even if the wages were small and the hours were long, since it was often hard to find work of any kind. (See pages 8-9.) A job in a shop or an office was considered a respectable and safe position. Although both girls and boys worked, girls usually left after marriage, and, as you will see, were advised to think about their jobs in a very different way.

> Boys are often put off from office work by the idea that the average office is dirty and dark and stuffy. That is a thing of the past. The modern offices that are springing up all over the country have masses of windows and are light and airy and they give the occupants the best possible chance of doing good work. Conditions of work, of course, vary. I suppose hours are, on an average, from nine in the morning till six at night, and wages start at fifteen shillings or sixteen shillings a week, and end up – for ordinary clerical work – at about £250 or £300 a year. I say 'for ordinary clerical work', but a boy can go a great deal further if he takes advantage of his early training and if he has got diligence and intelligence. . . . For instance, he might find he is interested in accountancy, company secretarial work, statistical analysis, or shipping and forwarding work. . . . So far I seem to have talked only about boys. What I have said applies to girls too. . . . But the positions open to girls in the modern office are quite different from the ones open to boys. The work that they are generally expected to do is shorthand and typewriting, and their ultimate goal is to become a secretary. (From a talk, "Varieties of Office Work" by J.F. McCartney, recorded in *The Listener,* 15 February 1933)

What do you learn from this about the way in which office conditions were changing in the 1930s?

IMPROVEMENTS IN HYGIENE

Employers were becoming aware that healthy and hygienic working conditions were essential both for efficiency and safety, especially where food production was involved.

> The drive for the clean-up in the dairy industry happened just after we got married and we went into what we called "Grade A" milk production, which was inspected by the County Council officials who even handed out prizes for the best production. We missed the prize by one point one year. I said to the Inspector, "Well, what have we done wrong?" He said, "Do you see that bucket over there? What do you do with it?" "We feed the calves with it." He answered, "It's no business there!" I had never thought about it – everything was polished and scrubbed, the floors were magnificent, the cows were washed and the dairy utensils sterilized. I'd got two young boys working for me and they were enthusiastic to win the prize – ten pounds and a certificate to stick up. I said to Bert, the younger boy, "Look at that – it shouldn't have been here!" and he kicked the bucket across the yard, which put paid to it for good! (Interview with Arthur Oakes, farmer, 1983)

What kind of work had the farmer and his helpers been doing to try to get their dairy in first class condition?

◁ *Offices at Dunston Soap Works, Tyne and Wear district, at the beginning of the 1930s. What can you learn about the kind of equipment and furniture in use?*

HEAVY AND DANGEROUS WORK

Certain occupations, such as coal-mining, involved working exceptionally hard in unpleasant conditions, with a great risk of injury. About one in every thousand miners was killed each year. Nowadays, powered equipment and strict safety measures have improved mining jobs considerably. George Orwell visited a mine to see for himself what went on; here he describes the work of the "fillers":

> The first impression of all, over-mastering everything else for a while, is the frightful, deafening din from the conveyor belt which carries the coal away. You cannot see very far, because the fog of coal dust throws back the beam of your lamp, but you can see on either side of you the line of half-naked kneeling men, one to every four or five yards, driving their shovels under the fallen coal and flinging it swiftly over their left shoulders. They are feeding it on to the conveyor belt, a moving rubber belt a couple of feet wide which runs a yard or two behind them.... It is impossible to watch the 'fillers' at work without feeling a pang of envy for their toughness. It is a dreadful job that they do, an almost superhuman job by the standards of an ordinary person. For they are not only shifting monstrous quantities of coal, they are also doing it in a position that doubles or trebles the work. They have got to remain kneeling all the while – they could hardly rise from their knees without hitting the ceiling – and you can easily see by trying it what a tremendous effort this means.... They are on the job for seven and a half hours, theoretically without a break, for there is no time 'off'.
> (*The Road to Wigan Pier*, 1937)

11

Home Life

WORKING-CLASS HOMES

Although many working-class families lived in distressing poverty, others were often secure and happy in their homes. George Orwell described his impressions of the people he visited, in *The Road to Wigan Pier*:

> In a working-class home . . . you breathe a warm, decent, deeply human atmosphere which it is not so easy to find elsewhere. . . . Especially on winter evenings after tea, when the fire glows in the open range and dances mirrored in the steel fender, when Father, in his shirt sleeves, sits in the rocking chair at one side of the fire reading the racing finals, and Mother sits on the other with her sewing, and the children are happy with a pennorth of mint humbugs, and the dog lolls roasting himself on the rag mat – it is a good place to be in.

Can you say in your own words what makes this such a cheerful and contented scene?

ROUTINE

Most married women stayed at home to look after their families. It was expected that childcare, housework and cooking would take up most of the day. A household manual gave this advice:

> When anyone is running a factory they map out every tiny detail, saying when the smallest and most important things shall be done and how and by whom. *It is just the same in planning a home. . . .* Draw up a plan labelled 'Weekly Jobs', and write down under each day its special task, such as 'drawing-room', 'silver', 'kitchen', 'washing' and so on. Then draw up a chart marked 'Daily Jobs', and write down in detail each thing, beginning, 'Put on the kettle, light fire and clear out ashes', and so on.
> (*Every Woman's Enquire Within*, edited A.C. Marshall, C. Arthur Pearson Ltd)

What does this tell you about the attitude which women were encouraged to have towards their housework?

THE COPPER

Very few families possessed a washing machine, and many boiled up their clothes and sheets in a "copper", a kind of large tank which could have a fire lit beneath it to heat the water it contained. Norma Deering, born in 1925, remembers her grandmother's wash house in Gillingham, Kent, where the copper was sometimes put to other uses:

> My grandmother had a little room with a copper which was built in with a slab surround and a lid. All the washing was done in that. Monday was washing day, and the kitchen was full of steam. There was a wooden 'dolly' to stir the washing with, and everything was boiled good and proper before it went out on the line. We lived nearby, and it was a family tradition that the Christmas puddings were made altogether at her house. Everybody stirred the puddings, and then we put them in basins, tied cloths over the top, and cooked them in the copper! (Interview with Norma Deering, 1983)

THE UPPER-CLASS HOME

Although the First World War had disrupted the traditional standards of the upper- and middle-class households, families who could afford it still employed servants to help in the home. A very rich family would have several servants, each with particular tasks. Here, the duties of the butler and the footman are described:

The Butler supervises menservants, is responsible for the wine cellar and table appointments, valuables and the silver in particular. He answers the door, announces visitors, attends to the telephone as well as waiting at table, and is responsible for the tidiness and cleanliness of the library and the billiard room . . .

The Footman is responsible for knives, boots, windows, lamps, and answering the door when the butler is not available. He makes up the fires and waits on the master of the house. A man with a knowledge of mechanics and electrical work is invaluable in the country house, for he can look after the electric lighting plant, electric lawn mower, renew fuses and attend to the car. (D.D. Cottington Taylor, *Good Housekeeping*)

Can you work out what all these jobs involve? How did the work of the 1930s footman and butler differ from those of the Victorian era?

THE PROBLEMS OF SOLID FUEL

Most homes still had coal fires, and often a solid fuel boiler or cooking range as well.

Our coalhouse was *inside* the house – it led off the kitchen. We could only afford one or two hundredweights a time at 1s 6d a bag, and when this had been dropped in the whole kitchen had to be scrubbed down to get rid of the film of coal dust. There was no such thing as a "vacuum sweep". When the chimney was swept, the soot went everywhere and again the sitting room had to be thoroughly cleaned. (Recollections written by Noel Leadbeater, 1983)

A working-class family from Cardiff, having tea. Do you think this might be a Sunday tea, and if so, why?

Children

Noel Leadbeater grew up in Birmingham. She had several brothers and sisters and her family was very poor. Noel was born in 1920, and by the early 1930s she was considered old enough to help with looking after the younger children. Here she remembers the games and expeditions they shared with other children in the neighbourhood.

Children were expected to amuse themselves. There were very few family outings, as large families were common and bus fares even at a penny or twopence each could not be afforded. A walk to the nearest park or perhaps a stream, with baby in the pram, two toddlers and several older children was a treat when an overworked mother could spare the time. A few sandwiches – banana or fishpaste – and a bottle of cold tea made a real feast.

We played marbles, tip-cat, flicking cigarette cards, hide and seek, hopscotch, all in their due seasons. Most children could not afford wooden hoops when that season came round but an old bicycle wheel with a tyre still on made a good substitute. In better-off families quite big girls – 11 or 12 – would play with dolls' prams.

Most of our games depended largely on imagination. A shop would be set up in the garden with a plank over a brick for scales. Stones were potatoes and dock leaves cabbages. The boys would play cricket but they seldom had a proper bat or wickets – just what a handy Dad could make. (Recollections written in 1983)

Why do you think the bigger girls might have enjoyed playing with dolls and prams?

A game of cricket in the street. What kind of clothes are the boys wearing?

Babies being aired in Kensington Gardens, London, February 1933. Some of the women were probably nannies. What do you notice about the style of prams in use?

MIDDLE- AND UPPER-CLASS FAMILIES

Children were brought up more strictly in these families than they are today, and many were looked after by nannies or servants. Even teenagers scarcely went out in the evenings, and schoolwork was expected to take priority.

We went to bed a lot earlier than children do today, at about half past seven or eight o'clock even when we were ten or eleven. We were allowed to read for a while, but it was considered "bad" for you if you didn't go to bed. There was unquestioning obedience not only in the schools but in the homes too. You never thought of arguing, or of saying, "I don't want to go to bed". On schooldays it was come home, have something to eat, do your homework and then go to bed. There was never any time for anything else. (Interview with Michael Deering, 1983)

CHILD PSYCHOLOGY

People began to think more carefully about whether there was a "right" and a "wrong" way to bring up children. One of the popular theories of the 1930s was that babies should be treated strictly from birth, with very little cuddling or comforting.

There is no doubt that from the day we first hold our baby in our arms, we should start teaching him unquestioning obedience.

No modern mother rocks her baby all night, or expects to be woken up frequently or during it. She knows that, so long as nothing is physically wrong with the child, she has only to turn him round, and he will not expect to be picked up, but will soon obey her unspoken command and settle off to sleep again. (From a talk, "Discipline and the Child" by Mrs St Aubyn, published in the *Radio Times*, 11 April 1930)

Schools

Free education in the 1930s was limited to Council Schools, which children attended from ages 5 to 14. A higher standard of education was available at the Grammar Schools (11-18 years), but most parents had to pay fees for this. Many children from the middle and upper classes went to private schools, either day or boarding. Although most education in the 1930s was very formal, with learning "drills" and strict discipline, in a few schools "progressive" new ideas were tried out, such as allowing children to follow activities and projects of their own choice.

A BIRMINGHAM COUNCIL SCHOOL

We had to sit very straight in our desks – which were often too small – arms folded *behind* our backs. A child who was late was usually caned – consequently if you thought you would be late you stayed at home and pretended you had been ill.

At playtime, as break was called, the teachers did not go into the staffroom as they do now, but remained at their desks. A cup of hot milk in the morning or tea in the afternoon was carried in carefully by a girl in the "top" class – the boys were never trusted with this chore. Two big girls washed up the cups later.

Girls and juniors shared one playground, while the big boys always had to use a smaller playground away behind the buildings. Boys did woodwork and science, while girls did cookery and needlework. Girls also had to learn how to launder. About twenty flat irons were put on a sheet of tin which was placed across gas jets. They had to be rubbed in sand, then on emery paper before using. The heat was tested by holding the iron (with a thick cloth over the handle) near one's hand. It was strictly forbidden to hold the iron near one's face, although every girl had seen her mother do this.

(Recollections written down by Noel Leadbeater, 1983)

What do you learn about the difference in the school routine for boys and girls?

A class of girls at a school in Rochester, Kent, in the early 1930s. Note the "gym slips" they wear, which were a typical feature of uniform.

"SPECIAL PLACES" AT GRAMMAR SCHOOLS

Children could take an exam before they entered Grammar School to try to win a "special place", which would mean that their parents paid less than the full fee or nothing at all for their education. Here are the results for some of the children who took an entrance exam to Okehampton Grammar School in 1938:

Sylvia Margaret Fretwell – To pay £4.10.0 per annum part tuition fees
Michael George Webber – Free Tuition
Roy Arthur Sildon – Free Tuition, half cost of travelling in County bus.

Sidney Bushe Hain – Full Fees
Leonard J Merrifield – Free Tuition, Railway Season Ticket, Books and £1 per term towards School Dinners
Horace Colin Headon – Free Tuition, Books, Railway Season Ticket and School Dinners.
(From the Minutes of a Governors' meeting of Okehampton Grammar School)

What extra benefits did some children receive as well as free tuition?

A COUNTRY SCHOOL

Here are some entries from the log book of Oakford village school, in Devon, written by the headmistress.

1931 – May 4th. About 200 bunches of primroses were brought to the school this morning, and sent by Miss G Anson and myself to four London schools.
May 15th – Owing to the heavy rain this morning only 46 children were present out of a possible 75.
June 3rd – This afternoon a visit was paid by Mr J H Hayes, chief attendance officer. He examined the duplicate registers [and] discussed the possibility of providing a conveyance for the long distance children of Mildon Cot road.
June 11th – Frederick H M_____ has to be excluded from school on suspicion of suffering from ringworm.
June 15th – Albert C_____ is excluded owing to ringworm.
July 14th – Dr Hosegood visited school today and examined the children.

One girl, Nancy S_____, was sent home in a verminous condition.
November 3rd (from a report made by His Majesty's Inspector) The provision of shoes and stockings for use in school when the weather is wet has undoubtedly benefited the health of the children. Many of the scholars have to walk a long distance, and better arrangements for their midday meal are very desirable.
1932 – Jan 6th. Ovens have been placed over the stoves – one in the Upper School and one in the Infants School. Children can now bring something to be warmed for their midday meal.

What particular problems arose as a result of this school's being in the country, and how did the teachers and inspectors try to solve them? (You will find a health problem shown up here, too, which was just as common in city schools!) And what special activity were the children able to take part in because they lived in a rural area? Can you think of any others they might have enjoyed which aren't mentioned here?

Clothes

There was a general desire for elegant and sophisticated clothes in the 1930s. This came partly as a reaction against the wild and daring fashions of the 1920s, when women wore very short dresses, and partly because in times of financial hardship, such as the 1930s, people often try harder to appear well-dressed and respectable. Nearly everyone, male and female, wore a hat or cap when going out, for instance, and men only sat in their shirtsleeves in the privacy of their own homes. Usually they wore a suit and tie, or jacket and trousers; even those with little money would try to have one suit for "Sunday best". For women, clothes were close-fitting and well-cut, with hem-lines coming below the knee. If you look through the other sections of this book you will find plenty of examples of the styles and variety of clothes worn. Many people still had their clothes made-to-measure, but there was a growing demand for a choice of ready-made garments. Poorer people often bought their clothes second-hand and would mend, darn or patch them rather than throw them away.

WOMEN'S CLOTHES

Matching jackets and skirts were tailored in pure wool tweed and were warm and cosy in winter, worn with hand-knitted or ready-made woollen jumpers, cardigans or "twin-sets". Leather coats, very soft, wool-lined and dyed attractive colours, were popular too and quite cheap at about £5.

For summer wear, there were the popular "Macclesfield" silk dresses, shirt-waister style, with multi-coloured delicate stripes. There were also cotton and linen dresses in plain, striped and floral materials.

Evening or afternoon dresses were often made of pure silk – crepe, chiffon, taffeta or velvet, cut on the cross to provide a fitting bodice and a flared skirt. "Ring" velvet was very fine and soft and so-called because a width of it could be pulled through a wedding ring.

Although most clothes were made of natural fibres, artificial silk and rayon were available, but these were used for the cheaper clothes. (Recollections written down by Kathleen Phillips, 1983)

A typical lady's outfit, from the catalogue of a London store. Note the popular fashion of wearing the hat tilted over one eye.

Some of the clothes that men would wear, from the Army and Navy Stores catalogue. Can you work out which descriptions go with which outfits, and also say whether they would be worn for work, sport or leisure?

SPORTS AND FLANNEL WEAR
MADE TO ORDER.

RIDING WEAR.
Jacket,
Vest and Breeches.
Smartly cut, in hard-wearing Tweeds.
Prices from .. £7 19 6
Riding Jacket only.
From .. £4 4 0
To .. £5 19 6
Tattersall Vest or Postboy Style.
From .. £2 10 0
Breeches or Jodhpurs, in Cavalry Twill or Bedford Cord.
From .. £4 4 0
To .. £1 15 0
POLO BREECHES.
In White Drill.
From .. £3 2 0

SHOOTING WEAR.
Patterns and Prices on application.

SPORTING JACKETS.
Made from the finest Scotch and Irish Tweeds.
From .. £3 3 0
Knickers only from £1 14 6

GREY AND WHITE FLANNEL TROUSERS.
Made in fine West of England Flannel.
From .. £1 12 0
To .. £2 5 0

BLAZERS.
Made in fine West of England Flannel. Single- and Double-breasted. Blue or White.
From .. £2 15 0
To .. £4 4 0

CLUB BLAZERS.
Prices on application. Reduced prices for quantities.
Embroidered Club Badges a speciality.

WHITE GABARDINE TROUSERS.
From .. £1 16 0
To .. £2 5 0

KNICKER SUITS.
Plus Four or the conservative style of Knicker.
Made in all the finest Scotch and Irish Tweed.
From .. £5 17 6
Harris Tweed specially obtained direct from the Crofters.
From .. £7 7 0

GREY FLANNEL SUITS.
Made in fine West of England Flannel.
From .. £5 15 0
To .. £8 5 0
Single- or Double-breasted. 2- or 3-button front.

GREY WORSTED FLANNEL SUITS.
Made in fine worsted Flannel.
From .. £6 12 6
To .. £8 5 0
Single- or Double-breasted. 2- or 3-button front.

ALL PRICES ARE SUBJECT TO MARKET FLUCTUATIONS

MEN'S SUITS

Burton's, the tailors, became famous for offering a made-to-measure suit at a price which the ordinary office worker could afford:

Burton's 45/– suit
4 guinea value suit to measure for 45/–. Unrestricted choice of over 500 new patterns.

A new suit – you deserve it after the winter; a new suit – a man feels brighter, younger, braver. A new style for every taste, a fit for every figure. New suitings surpassing anything Montague Burton's have ever prepared for man's delight. . . . Yorkshire Tweeds (the finest in the world), smooth-draping serges, new Worsteds, Scotch Tweeds, Irish Tweeds – what richness is yours, what luxury of material.

Strictly Personal
Your order is executed exactly to your own personal requirement. Your measurements are taken by experts, and each garment is cut and designed by skilled craftsmen for you alone.
(Advertisement in *News Chronicle*, 3 May 1935)

In what ways were Burton's trying to attract customers to order suits?

Manners

Proper "etiquette" was considered very important in the middle and upper classes; this meant knowing the right way to speak, behave and dress for different occasions. Most social events such as parties, dinners, weddings, dances and presentations were arranged quite formally, and guests were expected to understand the "rules" for each type of occasion so that they would not make embarrassing mistakes. A person who could manage this was thought "well-bred", and, indeed, had probably been trained to cope with social etiquette while growing up in an upper-class family.

WHAT TO WEAR

Hats and gloves were a "must" for formal occasions – such as attending Church, tea parties, even at formal lunch parties (when the hostess also wore a hat!) – and of course at Wimbledon, which was then something of a fashion parade. One's luggage always included a hat box – a round affair with a carrying strap.
(Recollections written down by Kathleen Phillips, 1983)

For most dinner parties and dances, evening dress would be required. Women would wear long dresses.

Evening dress for men consists of full dress with a tail-coat, or for less formal occasions of a dinner jacket. With a tail-coat a white waistcoat and tie are usually worn; but a black waistcoat and tie are the thing with a dinner-jacket. (*Every Woman's Enquire Within*)

A young couple at a Cambridge graduation ceremony. The man is wearing the correct clothes in which to receive his degree. What items of the young woman's clothing suggest that she has dressed formally to accompany him?

HOW TO BEHAVE

For those who were uncertain, books could be consulted to make sure that they could cope with the etiquette for a particular situation:

At Homes – It is customary for the hostess to receive her guests at the door of the principal room. Usually there is no formal entertainment, the company engaging in small-talk. Ladies retain their hats and wraps, but gentlemen are relieved of their outdoor things by the maid in the hall. Tea is served at a main table at one end of the room, the gentlemen waiting on the ladies, and handing round small sandwiches, cakes, etc.

Walking – A gentleman should always walk on the outside of a lady, i.e. between her and the kerb or traffic. If he meets a lady friend whilst walking, a gentleman lifts his hat with the hand farthest away from her. A tall gentleman should try to adjust his stride and pace to those of a short lady in whose company he may be. (*Every Woman's Enquire Within*)

What kind of people do you think might need to read about etiquette in books?

DEBUTANTES

It was the tradition that young ladies from aristocratic families were presented to the King and Queen at Court, usually when they were about seventeen or eighteen. They had to wear long white dresses, and ostrich feathers in their hair, and learn special curtsies and manners for the occasion. They were known as "debutantes" and the time of their presentation was called their "coming out". The "season" which followed would be an intense round of parties and dances, at which their parents hoped they might meet a suitable man to marry. In the 1930s the custom was enthusiastically maintained; in May 1934 alone, there were 3,000 dinner parties and 200 dances given for 300 debutantes.

Jessica Mitford described her presentation, which took place during the 1930s, in her autobiography, *Hons and Rebels* (1961):

Clambering finally out of the car, we stumbled through the rainy dark into a brightly lit, crowded corridor, filled with bare shoulders and the musty smell of rented ostrich feathers. More hours of inching . . . occasional gasps:
  'I think I'm going to faint!'
  'You *can't!* There isn't room.'
. . . Finally, the end of the road; a magnificent flunkey arranges our trains. . . . We are in the presence of what appear to be two large, stuffed figures, nodding and smiling down from their thrones like wound-up toys. One more river to cross: the curtsies, one to each of the stuffed figures, then backing away without stumbling until one is out of the Presence.

Although this was a very grand occasion, what do you think made it difficult for the girls taking part to enjoy it?

Building Houses and Flats

In the 1930s families no longer wanted large, gloomy Victorian houses, with extra rooms for servants. Homes needed to be compact and easy-to-run; people did not want elaborate plasterwork or fittings which would collect dust. Now that electricity and running water had become normal features of home life, it was expected that every new house would have a bathroom and be wired to take electric appliances and lighting. The most popular and desirable type of house was one that was individual in design, detached from its neighbours, with gardens both front and back.

Such a house was likely to cost upwards of £1,000, but a semi-detached house or bungalow could be bought for about £700. Many families sought privacy and respectability, and preferred to live in the suburbs rather than be too close to the unhealthy and overcrowded slum areas of the cities.

Purpose-built flats were often designed on a grand scale with flat roofs and streamlined exteriors. Were the flats for rent or for sale, and do you think someone would need a medium or a high income to live there? Remember that the average wage in the 1930s was about £4 a week. What special facilities are offered with these flats? ▷

The Deerings' house in Bromley, Kent.

A NEW HOUSE IN BROMLEY

Bromley was an up-and-coming town in the 1930s, when Norma Deering's father decided to buy a house there. The family could go for walks over the fields, and yet be in London in 20 minutes by train. You can see the house in the photograph; it was built in a popular style of the period known as "mock-Tudor". Can you find some illustrations of genuine Tudor houses and see in what way the two styles were similar?

My father had the house built in 1937, and it cost about £1,800. It was on a new and fairly high-class estate, where every house was built according to one of three basic plans, but each one was given a slightly different frontage. Ours had four bedrooms, a dining room, lounge, breakfast room, kitchen, bathroom and cloakroom, plus a garage. It had an oak-panelled hall which was the height of fashion! The kitchen was thought ultra-modern too, since it was fitted with a teak double-drainer sink, and cupboards all round the walls. But there were no work surfaces, only the kitchen table. As a special feature, there was an ironing board which let down out of a cupboard, but it always got in the way! There was a pantry, and an Ideal boiler which ran on coke and heated both the water and a radiator in the hall. That was really something, since in those days there was virtually no central heating! Most of the heating was from coal fires. Upstairs there was a sunken bath and an airing cupboard, and every room was wired up with one power point – all very modern! The windows had leaded lights, which were a status symbol then. The roof was tiled, the floors were properly boarded, and the ceilings made from lathe and plaster, not like the plaster board that is used today. (Interview with Norma Deering, 1983)

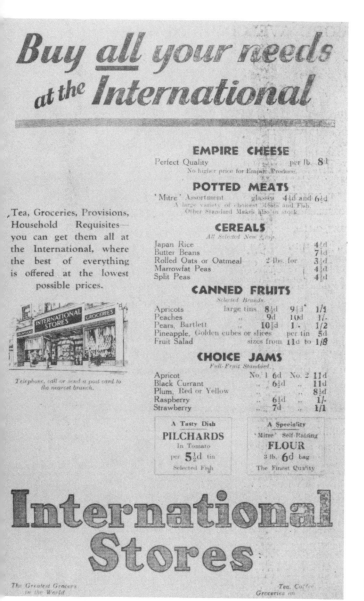

International Stores price list, 1931.

___DAILY MEALS___

We ate breakfast, lunch, afternoon tea and supper. For breakfast we had cereal – though there were only a few varieties on sale then, such as Post Toasties, Shredded Wheat and Force – and bacon and eggs, followed by toast and marmalade. We used to have our main meal at midday – meat, vegetables and so on. Then there was afternoon tea, which was a very civilized and middle-class meal. We'd drink tea and eat little pieces of bread and butter, or sandwiches, with scones, flapjacks or Scotch pancakes, followed by cakes and biscuits. Supper would be something like fish, or eggs, or maybe cold meats. We did eat more in those days, but don't forget that in the winter it was colder at home, because there was no central heating, and I think we ate more in order to keep warm.
(Interview with Norma Deering, 1983)

These were typical of the meals which would be eaten by a family with a reasonable income. Can you write a sample menu for a day, based on what is written here? Bear in mind that no frozen foods and not very many tinned or packeted foods were used then. You can find out from the International Stores price list about some of the convenience foods that *were* available.

FOOD ON A LOW BUDGET

Here are two extracts which describe the kind of food eaten by people who had very little money to spend. The first is from an unemployed house-painter and the second from an unemployed miner:

The chief article of our diet is bread. Margarine comes next. We invariably take sweetened condensed milk with our tea, a saving thereby being effected in the consumption of sugar; and we often use it to make rice-pudding. We usually purchase meat on Friday and Saturday evenings, cash being available on those days, and this being the time when butchers make an effort to sell their odds and ends. Fresh vegetables have been fairly cheap and these, together with cheap sausages, often form our principal meal on two or three days a week. (H.L. Bedes and R.S. Lambert, *Memoirs of the Unemployed,* Gollancz, 1934)

Life became a round of hateful sameness. A bit of bacon and a few tinned tomatoes on Friday when I drew the dole, then all the week through until Friday came again a constant procession of corned beef, cheap jam, margarine and potatoes. (G.A.W. Tomlinson, *Coal-Miner,* Hutchinson, 1937)

An advertisement for afternoon tea at an Edinburgh restaurant. The lettering and illustration are typical of the 1930s style. Having afternoon tea in the restaurant was very popular, especially after a shopping expedition.

What do you think about these diets? Can you think of anything they might need to make them more balanced? How does being "on the dole" affect the way these people shop and eat each week?

It was sometimes said that poor people spent too much of their money on sugary and unsuitable food. George Orwell pointed out that there was a reason for this:

When you are unemployed, which is to say when you are underfed, harassed, bored and miserable, you don't *want* to eat dull wholesome food. You want something a little bit 'tasty'. There is always some cheaply pleasant thing to tempt you. Let's have three pennorth of chips! Run out and buy us a twopenny ice-cream! Put the kettle on and we'll all have a nice cup of tea! . . . White bread-and-marg and sugared tea don't nourish you to any extent, but they are *nicer* (at least most people think so) than brown bread-and-dripping and cold water (George Orwell, *The Road to Wigan Pier*)

Do you agree with this?

You will find some other information about eating and shopping on a low budget in the sections on *Poverty and Unemployment* (pages 8-9) and *Shopping* (pages 26-27).

Shopping

DEPARTMENT STORES

There were many more department stores in existence than there are today. The staff were expected to attend to the customer's every need with courtesy and respect. Some were called "shopwalkers"; they were generally senior male staff whose duty was to see that everything was running as it should. Helen Forrester used to take her younger sister and brother into a large Liverpool department store for shelter, since their thin clothes and broken shoes gave them little protection from the wet and cold:

The accessories section of a Lincoln department store. From what you can see (display, furnishing, storage and so on), what can you tell about the ways in which buying and selling were conducted?

Avril's and my great enemies were the shopwalkers. Sometimes when we were cold, we would go into a big shop and skulk around the different departments until we became warm again. And then the shopwalker would pounce.

Shopwalkers always looked very imposing. They were usually elderly gentlemen dressed in stiff, white Victorian wing collars and black suits. They perambulated stiffly up and down the aisle of the shops, hands clasped behind their backs. They glared ferociously at the young girls and boys who served behind the counters. Then, with a slight bow, they would lend a courteous ear to customer enquiries . . .

I never argued with shopwalkers.

"What do you want?" they would snarl.

"I'm just looking," I would say loftily, exactly as I had heard people round me say.

The usual reply was, "You can look in the windows."

Then they would stride crossly to the nearest door and fling it open, and Edward, Avril and I would slink out like lost puppies.

(Helen Forrester, *Minerva's Stepchild*)

CARLTON ROAD, NOTTINGHAM

Here is a list from *Kelly's Directory of Nottingham* for 1936 of the shops and trades to be found in part of Carlton Road. Can you work out what all the abbreviations stand for? Are there any businesses which are not so common today? One is a trade specially connected with Nottingham – do you know which it is? Try to work out what any unfamiliar descriptions are, and also why it is likely, from the kinds of shops operating, that the street was in a poor area.

107	Albany works, Wrights & Dobson Bros. Ltd. lace bleachers & finishers
117	Newham J. H. & Sons, butchers
119	Wakefield Herbt. newsagt
121	Cooling H. J. fishmngr
123	Webber Percy, boot repr
125	Platts Alfd. grocer
127	Day Mrs. Ada, hardware dlr
129 & 131	Cragg & Shepherd, chemsts
133	Simpson Thos. butcher
151	Napper Mrs. Annie, news agt
153	Bakewell Christphr. boot mkr
155	Thompson John, butcher
157	Whiting Jn. & Sons Ltd. pawnbros
159	Marsden J. D. Limited. grocers
161	Ball Mrs. Annie, draper
163	Kirk Miss Ethel, hard confctnr
165	Bramley Jn. pork butcher
167	Turgoose Birkett, picture frame mkr
169	Dexter Thos. Albt. greengro
171	British & Argentine Meat Co. Limited, butchers
173	Baldwin Robert, grocer
177	Harrison Wm. confctnr
179	Greatrix F. & Son, fried fish dlrs
181	Stratton Mrs. Frances Mary, refreshment rooms
183	Morley Wltr. greengro
185	Bradley Miss Doris, milliner
187	Holmes Fredk. furniture dealer
189	Dawson Ernest, butcher
191	Whilde Jn. shopkpr
193	Dowlman Miss Mabel, boot mkr
195	Johns Miss Maud, fancy draper
197	Warner Wm. Gladstone, hardware dlr
199	Revis Jn. Hy. tobccnst
201	Wilkinson Harry, shopkpr
203	Pacey Rt. greengro
205	Sanderson Tom Ltd. tripe purveyors

A fleet of delivery vans working for Switzers, a large store in Dublin. Note that the drivers wear uniform.

For those living in a town or suburb, much of the family shopping could be done from home. The housewife would send in an order to a local shop, which would deliver the goods to her doorstep.

PERSUASIVE SELLING

A trend was growing to try to create more persuasive advertising and salesmanship. Manufacturers began to use "scientific" reasoning in their campaigns, which they hoped would impress the customer:

> Why *does* Persil wash things whiter than ordinary soaps and powders? Because of Persil's *oxygen*! Ordinary suds take the loose dirt away – and they stop at that. But Persil suds give out millions of tiny oxygen bubbles. These bubbles push right into the weave of the fabric. They go on gently cleansing and cleansing until there's not a trace of dirt or impurity *anywhere*.

(Advertisement in *News Chronicle*, 2 May 1935)

SMALL SHOPS

There were no supermarkets in the 1930s, and many more small shops in local streets which sold food and provisions. In poorer districts they served customers who could only afford to buy a little at a time:

> Stores which did this kind of splitting up of goods could with patience, make a lot more than those which did not. A sixpenny one-pound pot of jam, sold by the ounce at a penny an ounce, assured an excellent profit. Such shops were filled with black-shawled, unwashed women and skinny, barefoot children.

How much extra would the shopkeeper make on a pot of jam sold in this way?

Such shops were often badly kept:

> They are slovenly, dirty and inefficient. They only spoil the goods they offer for sale, especially if those goods, as they usually are, happen to be foodstuffs. . . . [They have] fly-blown windows and dark reeking interiors and blowsy proprietors. (J.B. Priestley, *English Journey*, 1934).

Law and Order

Police patrolling of the streets was usually done on foot. The most common types of trouble that the police had to deal with "on the beat" involved drunkenness, fighting or theft. One job which took up a great deal of their time was "point duty", which meant directing the traffic at busy road junctions. (Look at pages 32-33 to find out why this was necessary.)

Policemen were paid a reasonable, but not over-generous wage, of about £200 a year, plus extra for rent, but conditions in police stations were often difficult and the men had to work awkward shift systems which prevented them from enjoying a normal social or family life, and often provoked health problems for them.

ON DUTY IN LONDON

Here an English policeman tells a French policeman what it is like being on "point duty" in central London, and goes on to explain why the English police work unarmed:

> **Lots of foreigners come and ask things ... and they seem to think we know everything, not only how to get to places, but what to see in London, where to stay, where to eat, where to drink, how old the Prince of Wales is, and whether Broadcasting House is Buckingham Palace. They seem to forget that controlling traffic is our job.**
>
> **We are unarmed. I have never spoken to a constable yet who thought we should carry revolvers. We think it would be an encouragement for burglars to carry arms. We have our truncheons, of course, but they are very seldom used. We certainly don't look upon a policeman's job as dangerous here, and we certainly don't get any extra allowance for it.** (*The Listener*, 12 April 1933)

Do you think policemen of today would share these views? Do you think a policeman's job now is any more dangerous than it used to be in the 1930s?

STREET BATTLES

Unfortunately, there were occasional major battles between police and crowds. Early in the 1930s this sometimes happened when unemployed people came together to march in angry protest about lack of work and money. In 1931 Max Cohen witnessed a demonstration that turned into a riot in a town in north west England. The protesters had gathered to complain about a Government scheme to cut down the money they received on the dole and to introduce the Means Test (see pages 8-9):

New police recruits being instructed in "point duty".

It seemed as though a mighty flood of people stretched down the street, into the distance, as far as the eye could see. I had never seen such a large crowd.... Suddenly the foot police, with batons drawn, began to move forward towards the demonstration. Those at the head of the crowd moved towards the police. I saw men closing with the police, and police slashing out with their batons. A furore of noise raged over the crowd – boos, yells and shouts of rage. Soon a pitched battle was raging. Unemployed and police fought desperately together. Men lay unconscious on the ground. Slogan-boards flew through the air, the sticks to which they were nailed cracked like rifles. (Max Cohen, *I was One of the Unemployed,* 1945)

What seems to have changed the march into a fight? Can you think of any possible reasons why the police failed to prevent matters getting out of hand?

Fascist meetings had caused such violence and distress through their provocative behaviour (see page 44) that at the end of 1936 Parliament agreed to pass a law banning organizations such as these whose members dressed and acted in a military fashion. The most prominent Fascist group in Britain was the British Union of Fascists, led by Sir Oswald Mosley, which had about 40,000 members. Some Members of Parliament had been asking for such a law for several years and were concerned that the Home Secretary and the police were not doing enough to stop the trouble.

June 1936
Mr Montague ... asked the Secretary of State for the Home Department ... the number of mounted and other police drafted into Finsbury Park yesterday on the occasion of a Fascist demonstration and upon whom falls the cost of these ... [and] whether he is aware that the only violence exhibited was that of Sir Oswald Mosley's supporters; that the demonstration was organised in military fashion with uniformed men ... and military orders given by loudspeakers though loudspeakers of a perfectly peaceful rival meeting were ordered to be toned down ... Why is it that the police protected the Fascist military band, which was playing in the park?
Sir J Simon – I altogether dispute the allegation that the police protected anybody. (*Hansard Parliamentary Proceedings*)

What was Mr Montague especially worried about in connection with the police? Why do you think groups behaving like armies can be a threat to the peace of the community?

◁ *Another struggle between police and unemployed men who were marching through High Holborn, London, in 1931. The police are trying to seize the man's banner.*

29

There was no National Health Service in the 1930s, which meant that most medical and dental treatment had to be paid for by the patient. Poor people would often avoid calling out a doctor for as long as possible, as they found it hard to pay his fees. There were insurance schemes available, for which you paid a certain sum of money each week and which guaranteed that your medical bills would be met. Hospital treatment was less common then, and patients were nursed at home as far as possible. Some hospitals were publicly run and others were voluntary, which meant that they were funded by charity. Often local people worked hard to try to raise money for a voluntary hospital in their area. During the 1930s, though, there was a policy of bringing more and more hospitals into the "Public Health" section. The number of beds available in these hospitals was 38,000 in 1933 but it had risen to 60,000 by 1939.

SLIM *for* Health and Beauty SAFELY *and* SURELY — USE **NATEX REDUCING FOOD**

NO DRUGS NO THYROID JUST NATURAL

Actors, Actresses, Mannequins, Doctors, Nurses, etc., all praise NATEX REDUCING FOOD, because it is purely vegetable and because it reduces superfluous fat Nature's way. You can't over-slim with NATEX, because it's natural. As your weight goes down, your health is built up by the vitamins and organic salts of the vegetables from which NATEX REDUCING FOOD is prepared.

2/-
5/6
and 9/6
from
ALL CHEMISTS

SEND FOR FREE SAMPLE, TO

MODERN HEALTH PRODUCTS, LTD., 17, Natex House, Langham Street, W.1

This advertisement suggests that some people had been using harmful methods to slim. What were they?

As you can see from the wording, attention was now being paid to the composition of food and to the balance of minerals and vitamin salts in diet as a way of maintaining health. Sometimes advice given was amusing, as in this article on how to cook cabbage:

"Many housewives will be glad to hear of experiments on cabbage-cooking that have recently been reported.

"The problem was to find out the method of cooking cabbage which left the largest amount of vitamins over in the cabbage. The first experiment was to find out which was better – to boil finely shredded cabbage, or to boil the cabbage in quarters.

"The result proves that you will get the largest amount of Vitamin C . . . if you shred the cabbage, provided that you drink the cabbage water as well . . ."
(Picture Post, *19 November 1938*)

HOSPITAL TREATMENT FOR THE POOR

Very often those seeking free medical care in hospital had to suffer uncomfortable conditions, and, although some doctors and staff were sympathetic, others treated such people as inferior. In the early 1930s Helen Forrester was taken to a Liverpool hospital by her mother, suffering from an acute illness brought on by a poor and inadequate diet.

> ... The shabby crowd awaited the opening of the Outpatients' Department. A cold wind fluttered the stained raincoats of the men and the bundly overcoats of the women, some of whom hugged beshawled children ...
>
> Every so often I would feel faint and would start to reel and Mother would pin me against the building's wall so that I did not fall. After waiting about half an hour ... the door was opened ... and the motley crowd poured in, elbowing each other in an effort to be first.
>
> We found ourselves in a large waiting room with lines of wooden benches, and we sat down, not sure what we were supposed to do next.
>
> I fainted against Mother's shoulder and, when I came round, I heard an angry rumbling from the waiting crowd. Apparently, Mother had asked a passing nurse for a glass of water and the girl had said coldly that it was not necessary, that I would come round quick enough. (Helen Forrester, *Minerva's Stepchild*)

What do you think could perhaps have been done to improve the way these patients were treated?

STAYING HEALTHY

Interest was growing in how to keep healthy through the right sort of diet, exercise and tonic medicine. It was fashionable to think that you would become ill if you did not go to the lavatory regularly. Children were dosed each week with a laxative medicine – more often if they seemed bad-tempered!

> "What would you do with such a naughty boy, Nurse?"
>
> "Don't scold him, Mrs Hardy. He doesn't look well. Are you sure he is not constipated? Whenever a child is cross and peevish I look at the tongue. If it is coated, or if the breath is disagreeable, I know at once what is wrong. I always give 'California Syrup of Figs.' That moves the bowels in a few hours and cleanses the system."
>
> (Advertisement in *News Chronicle*, 30 April 1935)

THE DENTIST

> The dentist was the great dread. It was very painful, and you spent all your school holidays going to the dentist. As soon as the school term was over you had your first visit. He would only do one filling at a time, and you didn't have any injections for them. I had a broken tooth which was crowned, and I remember him drilling upwards to kill the nerve. I saw stars – I nearly blacked out! (Interview with Michael Deering, 1983)

Road traffic increased considerably during the 1930s. Previously, most long-distance travel had been by rail and quite a lot of local transport – especially delivery of goods – by horse-drawn vehicles. Owning a car had been an expensive luxury. But now a new car could be bought for £100, and a second-hand one for as little as £10, putting car-ownership within the reach of many more families. More lorries began to take over the transporting of goods, and coach travel started to offer a cheaper alternative to trains for long journeys. Trams ran in many towns and cities, but since they ran on a track fixed into the road, they became increasingly dangerous in heavy traffic. They could not pull out to avoid a hazard or make way for large lorries and so local authorities began to phase them out. Main roads and city roads became crowded and chaotic, for there had been few rules to cope with motorists in the past. Mr Hore-Belisha, the Minister for Transport, introduced traffic lights, roundabouts, pedestrian crossings and one-way streets, and a 30 mph speed limit was imposed in 1934 in urban areas. New by-passes and city ring roads were completed too, to ease the flow of traffic.

TRAINS

Here is part of the Somerset and Dorset Railway timetable for 1931. There were many more local stations and lines which passengers could use in the 1930s. Try to trace this route on a map (you will need one that is large-scale, such as an Ordnance Survey or motoring map), noting how close together some of the stations lie and how small the villages are which they serve. From the timetable, can you find out another important way in which trains were used?

DOWN – BRANCH LINE.

All services PASSNGR (p.m.) except 12B: MILK & PERISHBLS to Templecmbe.

STATIONS.	8B arr.	8B dep.	9B arr.	9B dep.	10B arr.	10B dep.	11B arr.	11B dep.	12B arr.	12B dep.	13B arr.	13B dep.	14B arr.	14B dep.	15B arr.	15B dep.
Burnham-on-Sea	S	1 45	..	2 0	S	2 35	..	3 10	..	..	..	5 10	S	5 35	..	6 30
Highbridge Wharf	..	..	..	..	..	..	..	..	..	..	..	..	..	..	..	..
„ Goods	..	..	..	..	..	..	..	..	..	..	..	..	..	..	..	..
„ Statn.	1 50	..	2 5	..	2 40	..	3 15	3 19	F	4 0	5 15	5H20	5 40	..	6 35	6 45
Bason Bridge	..	..	..	..	..	..	3 23	3 24	4 4	4 22	5 24	5 25	..	..	6 49	6 50
Edington Junction	..	..	..	..	..	..	3 30	..	..	4 28	5 31	..	..	..	6 56	..
Bridgwater	..	1 10	..	..	..	..	..	3 D 5	..	..	..	5 10	..	..	..	6 30
Bawdrip Halt	1 15	1 16	..	..	..	..	3 10	3 11	..	..	5 15	5 16	..	..	6 35	6 36
Cossington	1 19	1 20	..	..	..	..	3 14	3 15	..	..	5 19	5 20	..	..	6 39	6 40
Board's Siding	..	..	..	..	..	..	..	..	..	..	..	..	..	..	..	..
Edington Junction	1 26	..	..	..	..	..	3 21	..	..	..	5 26	..	..	..	6 46	C
Edington Junction	..	..	..	..	..	..	..	3 32	4 40	..	..	5 34	..	..	..	6 58
Shapwick	..	..	..	..	..	..	3 37	3 38	4 44	4 50	5 39	5 40	..	..	7 3	7 4
Ashcott	..	..	..	..	..	..	3 42	3 43	4 54	4 59	5 44	5 45	..	..	7 8	7 9
Glastonbury	..	..	..	..	..	..	3 49	3 57	5 5	6 5	5H51	..	..	..	7 15	7R21
West Pennard	..	..	..	..	..	..	4 6	4 10	6 16	6 31	..	..	..	..	7 30	7 31
Pylle	..	..	..	..	..	..	4 17	4 18	6 39	6 50	..	..	..	..	7 38	7 39
Evercreech Jun. N.	..	..	..	..	..	..	4 22	..	..	6 54	..	..	..	..	..	7 42
Evercreech Jun.	..	..	..	..	..	..	4 23	..	6 55	7 30	..	..	..	..	7 44	..

Passenger. "THAT WAS A POLICEMAN! Now you'll get into TROUBLE."
Driver. "WHY, IS THERE SOME SUPERSTITION ABOUT IT?"

Punch, *16 March 1932. Regulations were tightened up in the 1930s because motorists had been used to having their own way for too long! What other form of transport can you see in this cartoon? If you look through the other sections of this book, you will see some more examples of 1930s vehicles.*

COACH TRAVEL

The Victoria Coach Station, in London, was completed in 1931 as a terminus for long-distance coach travel. On the trains, there were different classes of travel, but on coaches it was the same for everyone. J. B. Priestley is a writer who took a journey around England in 1933 with the intention of writing about how people lived and worked in different areas. Sometimes he made use of coaches to travel from one town to another.

There seems to be a motor coach going anywhere in this island. . . . I was astonished at its speed and comfort . . . these new motor coaches . . . offer luxury to all but the most poverty-stricken. They have annihilated the old distinction between rich and poor travellers. (*English Journey*, 1934)

ACCIDENTS

There was growing concern about road safety:

The startling results of the work of the Research Department of the National 'Safety First' Association regarding accidents in the roads and streets of England and Wales make melancholy reading, and show the terrible toll of human life that is daily taken by road traffic. The total number of persons killed in the six months July to December 1932 is given as 3129 . . . the most fated hours in practically every month were those after dark. . . . It is to be noted that 'dazzle' lights, or, at the other extreme, inefficient lighting, were the most frequently reported as the contributory cause of night accidents. (*Illustrated London News*, 13 May 1933)

In 1932, July-December, there were 2.2 million vehicles on the roads and 3,129 fatal accidents. In 1980, July-December, there were 19.2 million vehicles and 3,162 fatal accidents. Can you work out which was, in fact, the more dangerous period for road travel?

Country Life

THATCHING HAY RICKS

Far less machinery was used on farms in the 1930s than now and so a great deal of work was done by hand, or with the help of horses. When hay was made, there were no machines to bale it, so it was built into ricks, which were thatched to protect them from the weather.

The hay was put into the rick and allowed to settle for about three weeks to let the heat go out. Then I would pluck the sides of the rick, pulling out all the straggly bits, making it all as level as possible, and bringing it up to a point at the top. I'd take good straight pieces of wheat straw, soak them in water, and tie them into a bundle which I'd carry up on my back, and slip in behind the fork. I'd start thatching on the right hand side of the rick, sticking in thatch pegs in rows and tying cords along them to keep the thatch in place. Thatch pegs were often made in the winter days, from willow sticks which were nice and straight. When I saw a rick well-made it was beautiful, the sides clipped, all trimmed as though it had had its hair cut! You knew you were doing a job in which there was art. I didn't realize it was art until now, these latter years when there is no art. (Interview with Arthur Oakes, farmer, 1983. His farm in the 1930s was near Coventry.)

Arthur Oakes at work thatching a rick. Which details that he mentions can you pick out in the picture?

THE FARM KITCHEN

In 1936, T. Hennell published a book called *Change in the Farm,* in which he recorded many of the old ways of farm life which he thought were about to disappear. Here is his description of a typical farmhouse kitchen:

The kitchen is the largest and most comfortable room in the house, and on Sundays and holidays, when left to themselves, the family take possession of it for meals. It has a brick floor, lime-washed walls, and plain wooden table, chairs, cupboards, flour-bin and dresser; the last furnished with enough blue and white crockery to serve a regiment. The kitchen-clock and a frame worked by pulleys from the ceiling, to dry clothes before the fire, complete the essential furniture. The oven range is enormous; on it, beside the food of the household, are cooked the potatoes and meal for the poultry, pigs and calves. (E P Publishing, 1977 reprint)

A family from Cumbria in their kitchen in 1935. How does it compare with the description? What do you learn about the working clothes that the men are wearing? Notice the traditional way in which bacon is stored by hanging it from the ceiling.

DAILY LIFE

Country ways were often old-fashioned, since transport was difficult and services such as electricity were slow to reach rural areas.

> Many roads were not made up; they were just rock. Most people went about by horse and cart or on foot – children often walked six miles each way to school. Some folks would only go to the local town once every three months, to stock up on provisions such as flour and sugar. Bread was often made at home, and the lighting in our house was from oil lamps, which had to be kept trimmed and filled. (Interview with Enid Oakes, farmer's wife, 1983)

THREATS TO VILLAGE LIFE

In the 1920s and '30s there was a building boom, and great numbers of new houses, shops and factories were erected. Villages within easy reach of large towns and cities were especially likely to expand, and their inhabitants worried that the character of the village and the traditional way of life would be spoilt:

> Sir – This village of Lingfield is fortunate in possessing a charming group of old buildings on the south side of the fine old church. . . . Opposite this group of buildings is a series of three fields with a footpath leading down to the station in the valley. The station is hidden, but, adjacent to the farthest of the three fields . . . can be seen the gables of New Place, a charming stone house of the 17th century. . . . Thus the view both to and from New Place is an extremely pleasant one and at present free and uninterrupted and unusually rural for a Surrey village only 26 miles distant from London. It is now proposed to erect in the Upper Field . . . a cinema and a car park, and very many of the inhabitants of the village, including myself, have petitioned against such a proposal, on the ground that it will ruin the most charming part of the village . . . (Letter to the Editor, *Country Life*, 30 May 1936)

Why do you think this village might have been particularly attractive to developers?

Cinema and Radio

Until 1927 all films had been silent, but after this the "talkies" arrived. The cinema rapidly became the most popular place to go for an afternoon or evening out. Many new, sumptuous "Picture Palaces" were built with luxurious fittings and plush seats and it was often warmer and more comfortable to sit in the cinema than at home.

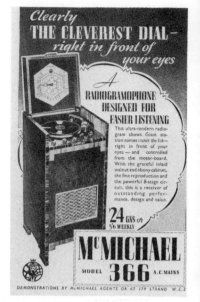

An advertisement from 1936.

CINEMAS IN CAMBRIDGE

Here is an entry from the *Kinematograph Year Book* of 1934 giving details of the cinemas in Cambridge. You will be able to see how much or how little a seat cost and how many people some of the cinemas could hold. Today, the population of Cambridge is around 100,000, and there are about four cinemas in use. How does that compare with the position in 1934?

CAMBRIDGE (CAMBS.), Pop. 66,803

CENTRAL CINEMA (WE), 21, Hobson Street. – Controlled by Union Cinema Co., Ltd., . . . London, W.1. Phone, Gerrard 6363. Booked at H.O. 1,100 seats. Continuous. Prices, 8d. to 2s. 5d. Proscenium width, 25 ft. Phone, Cambridge 13. Station, Cambridge, L.N.E.R. and Film Transport.

COSMOPOLITAN CINEMA (BTH), Market Passage. – Prop., Cosmopolitan Cinemas, Ltd., . . . Cambridge. 296 seats. Open during University Terms only. Four shows daily. Booked at Hall by N. Openshaw Higgins. Prices, 1s. to 2s. Proscenium width, 24ft. Stage, 27 ft. deep. Two dressing-rooms. . . .

KINEMA (WE), Mill Road. – Prop., Pointer & Coulson. 498 seats. Booked at Victoria Cinema. Continuous from 6.30. Mat., Sat. Two changes weekly. Prices, 5d. to 1s. 3d. Station, Cambridge, L.N.E.R.

NEW CINEMA (WE). – Controlled by Union Cinema Co., Ltd., . . . London, W.1. Phone, Gerrard 6363. 900 seats. Booked at H.O. Station, Cambridge, L.N.E.R.

PLAYHOUSE (BA), Mill Road. – Controlled by Union Cinema Co., Ltd., . . . 800 seats. Booked at H.O. Continuous Prices, 7d. to 2s. . . .

RENDEZVOUS CINEMA (RCA), Magrath Avenue. – 800 seats. . . . Continuous. Two changes weekly. Prices, 7d. to 1s. 9d. Proscenium width, 23 ft. Café and Dance Hall attached. . . .

TIVOLI (BA), Chesterton Road. – Controlled by Union Cinema Co., Ltd., . . . 500 seats. Booked at H.O. Continuous from 2.30. Prices, 6d. to 1s. 10d. . . .

VICTORIA CINEMA (WE), Market Hill. Prop., Pointer & Co., Ltd., . . . Cambridge. 1,500 seats. Booked at Hall. Continuous from 2.30. Two changes weekly. Prices, 6d. to 2s 4d. Phone, Cambridge 2677. Café attached. . . .

YOUNG PEOPLE AND THE CINEMA

Children were catered for in the film world, but obviously there was some concern as to whether the cinema was good for them. The writer of the next extract is trying to soothe parents' worries – can you tell what kind of worries they might be?

> Can our young people still transplant themselves to and lose themselves in a world of poesy and pixies, a world where their toys . . . come to life and the Little People leave their lovely, invisible land to mingle with the mortals?
>
> If they can – and I hope they can – where better shall they find the way to fairyland than in the cinema? The camera is a magician at whose bidding the boundaries of hard fact evaporate and the supernatural becomes as real, convincing. . . . An excellent selection of fairy tales – Ludwig Berger's 'Cinderella', 'The Toy Parade' . . . 'The Wedding of the Painted Doll', Bonzo and Mickey Mouse cartoons, the whole reinforced with animal and nature studies . . . will be shown during the whole of January at the enterprising Little Academy Cinema in Oxford St.
> (*Illustrated London News*, 2 January 1932)

THE BBC

The BBC broadcast a selection of comedy, drama, music (dance band and classical), news and talks. *The Children's Hour*, on between about 5 and 6pm every day, was popular with younger listeners. During the '30s "live" coverage of sports and news began, which brought in completely new possibilities.

> Among outstanding incidents in this actuality reporting may be mentioned the report of the Crystal Palace fire by an observer who was actually in the blazing building with the firemen, a report from inside a gas-filled chamber by an observer who had a microphone inside his gas-mask, and a broadcast from the banks of the Mississippi at Memphis while the floods were at their height. During this last broadcast the shouts and songs of the workers, the sound of sandbags being flung down, the lapping of the water against the bank and the noise of motor-boats on the river could be heard behind the speaker. (*BBC Handbook*, 1937)

What do this and Nancy Sharman's description (below) tell us about the new opportunities which radio brought to people's lives? Can you think of any others?

RADIO IN THE HOME

There was no television service at this time, and radio was the favourite form of home entertainment. More and more people bought a "wireless" set, so-called because the radio waves were transmitted through the air rather than along cables, although, in fact, the sets had both aerials and electric wires to be plugged in.

> Uncle Joe bought a wireless from Curry's for some money down, and then an instalment of sixpence a week. Our excitement was truly electric! Mum had a pink glow in her cheeks and we children were getting under Uncle's feet. He unwrapped the shiny black-and-white set, and shushed us up while he read the instructions. You could have heard the proverbial pin drop. One end of the sideboard was cleared and the wireless was placed on it as reverently as if it had been the Crown Jewels. There was a great length of wire called an aerial. . . . Uncle connected it up. 'Hey Presto!' Music came out. . . . We were, indeed, entering the electric age. (Nancy Sharman, *Nothing to Steal*)

PUTTING ON A SHOW

People enjoyed making a lot of their own entertainment. Local music, drama and light opera societies were especially popular:

> **Many of our evening activities consisted of things run by, or connected with, the church. The church provided so much, with a tennis and badminton club, socials, and amateur dramatics. We used to produce plays and general shows singing popular songs of the day, often combining a dance routine with some monologues and sketches. We "toured" with these productions around local places in a bus, doing "one night stands". This is a photo of our Harleston Revellers, in a production called "Harleston Follies"!**

(Recollections written down by Betty Owen, 1983)

Betty Owen was 16 at the time this picture was taken. She was living for a period with her uncle and aunt in the small town of Harleston, in Norfolk.

DANCES

Going out to a dance was a favourite activity for young people and married couples. Not all were held in the evening — some were afternoon "tea-dances", with a "Palm Court" Orchestra. Parents often preferred their daughters to go to one of these rather than be out late at night. Often a party of friends went together, having booked a table where they could sit and have refreshments when not dancing. Good manners were considered very important, and it was thought rude to refuse a dance if asked.

> *Popular Dances.* **To-day the dances most in fashion for the ballroom are the fox-trot, waltz, tango and quick-step....**

COMEDY THEATRE

BUSMAN'S HONEYMOON

A New Detective Comedy
by
DOROTHY L. SAYERS and M. ST. CLARE BYRNE

ACT. I

The Living Room at Talboys, 9.30 a.m. on a Wednesday morning
in October.

ACT II

The same, 1.30 p.m. the same day.

ACT III

Scene I.   The same, Thursday evening.

Scene II.   The same, Friday morning.

Every detective plot turns on three problems—
MEANS, MOTIVE, OPPORTUNITY.

The major clues for solving one of these are presented in the First Act.
Act II provides the material for the solution of another.
Act III, Scene I, adds enough evidence about the remaining problem [to
suggest the solution.
Can you anticipate the PROOF demonstrated in the last scene? If you are
not quite sure think back to the first Act.

From a programme for a play put on at the Comedy Theatre, London, in 1937. Detective stories had become very popular in the 1920s and 1930s and this one was turned into a play. How are the programme notes trying to help members of the audience who are not used to detective "thrillers"?

TOWN CHILDREN IN WINTER

In the winter only the rougher children played in the road – indoors there was nearly always a small coal fire and a large table to sit round for Ludo, Snakes and Ladders, Happy Families, Snap or card games. We swapped comics among friends, such as *The Magnet, Girl's School Friend, The Rainbow, Bubbles, The Gem* and *Hotspur.* (Recollections written down by Noel Leadbeater, 1983)

Good manners and the comfort of others form the basis of dancing deportment. The man should not attempt to indulge in fancy steps of his own; it generally means interfering with other couples dancing. Modern dancing is progressive, and failure to keep moving round the floor by trying some variation inevitably holds up others. (*Every Woman's Enquire Within,* Pearson Ltd, *c.* 1937)

Could you write a light-hearted description of some badly-behaved dancers at a Tea Dance?

COUNTRY ENTERTAINMENT

We used to gather in people's houses for parties – about 12 or 15 of us. We'd play card games like "Halfpenny Nap", and "Newmarket", or else we'd sing songs around the piano. Afterwards we'd have a feast! (Interview with Enid Oakes, farmer's wife, 1983)

Why do you think country people might have had more "get-togethers" than trips to the cinema or to dances? Look at the section on "Country Life" (pages 34-35) if you are not sure.

Outdoor Recreation

PICNICS

More and more families were now buying cars, till by the end of the 1930s about one family in every ten owned a car. This made it easy for many people to go into the country for a picnic at weekends.

> **Motorists are asked not to take their garden trowels with them in their cars to uproot ferns and flora from the hedgeside and woods, however keen they may be to add these to their own gardens. Also leaving glass bottles on commons and similar places has been the cause of many fires which have destroyed acres of lovely heaths. Therefore, both new and old car-owners are asked to leave no trace of their pleasurable halts for meals in our picturesque spots. . . . Picknicking is made very easy nowadays for motorists, as so many handy and compact appliances are available. Tea outfits and luncheon baskets, folding tables and chairs and non-breakable crockery, are to be obtained at very small cost now compared to former years. One can take advantage of the exhaust heat of the engine to boil up the tea kettle, for example. This method is safer than using methylated spirits or petrol for a fire. It is done by the kettle being provided with an adaptor, which can be fitted just below the exhaust manifold so that the burnt gases from the engine circulate around the special kettle.** (*Illustrated London News*, 25 March 1933)

Why might we now think this last suggestion unsafe? What problems are highlighted in this extract connected with an increased number of visitors to the countryside?

There was a growing movement in favour of open-air exercise and activity in the 1930s. "Keep Fit" became a popular slogan, and the Government tried to organize local sessions of sport and exercise, known as "Physical Culture". Fresh, country air was considered good for one's health, partly because the air of urban areas was still heavily polluted with smoke. Walking, camping and cycling were favourite activities. "Hiking" was the word used for long walks in the country; hikers of both sexes usually wore shorts and carried rucksacks on their backs. Nearer to home, tennis clubs became immensely popular, partly because they offered an opportunity for young men and women to meet and get to know each other.

CAMPING

Although most people used canvas tents to sleep in while camping, a new idea was adopted which allowed a slightly more comfortable trip.

Railway Camping Coaches. **Each of our railway companies now arranges for coaches to be stationed at sidings in the beauty-spots served by its particular system. The coaches are fully equipped so that they become what are virtually bungalows on wheels. They contain living and sleeping quarters and are complete with kitchen utensils, cutlery, crockery, linen, bedding and so forth. The majority of the coaches accommodate six persons and the terms vary from £2 10s to £4 per week, according to the size of the coach and the season of the year. . . . As the demand is considerable, reservations should be made several months in advance.** (*Every Woman's Enquire Within*)

"Come, on wings of joy we'll fly
To where my bower hangs on high;
Come, and make thy calm retreat
Among green leaves and blossoms sweet."

By GENERAL

(left) A party of young students enjoy a camping holiday. Compare this genuine photograph with the picture of the ideal picnic issued as an advertisement (above). Why would a bus company (General) have wanted to persuade people to have tea in the open air?

41

Holidays

SEASIDE HOLIDAYS

A week at the seaside was the favourite form of family holiday in the 1930s, with accommodation in a boarding-house or in rented rooms. In *Every Woman's Enquire Within,* there is a section called "Our Coast Resorts" which is designed to help the reader choose where to go. Here is the description of Blackpool:

> **Blackpool extending for about 7 miles along a bracing, windswept sea-front, is known the world over for its gaiety; but all its lively, boisterous, good spirits are built upon a solid foundation, for the place is a hundred-per-cent health resort. . . . Here the very air brings vim, and the making of amusement is a business, so there is always something to do! . . . There seems room for everyone, even in a place to which the railway company brings in a single day as many as 100,000 people.**
>
> **To pass muster at Blackpool, everything has to be of the very best, and this applies particularly to the indoor amusements at the Tower, Winter Gardens, Palace, Grand Theatre, Opera House, and cinemas. There are three piers, and the daily programme of events is unequalled anywhere . . .**
>
> **Among the countless attractions at Blackpool is the Open-Air Bath at South Shore . . . which provides aquatic sport for hundreds of thousands every season. A feature of this great resort is the illuminations in September and October, when the entire front is decorated with hundreds of thousands of electric lights, with working devices, kaleidoscopic signs, and novel effects.**

How do you think most people travelled to Blackpool? What kinds of amusements and activities did they enjoy there?

HOLIDAY CAMPS

In 1937 the first holiday camp was opened by Billy Butlin, and others quickly sprang into existence. The price for full accommodation and entertainment could be as little as 45/– per person per week.

> **Just before the war we tried out a holiday camp. We had a little chalet and I remember Dad being a bit put out because he said he couldn't get out of bed without putting his feet out of the window! It was very tight! But we children thought it was marvellous – there was a swimming pool, and games which you could join in or not, as you wanted, such as quoits, tennis and miniature golf. In the evenings they had dances, with the good old-time dancing with waltzes and foxtrots. They had cinema shows, but I don't remember us children doing a lot in the evenings, since we went off to bed at eight o'clock. They had competitions – they held a photographic competition and I had a little Brownie box camera with which I took a picture of some ducks on the water and won a prize! There was also a beauty contest for men. My father and his brother went into the parade dressed up in their wives' swimsuits!**
> (Interview with Norma Deering, 1983)

A day on the beach at Southend. Southend was a popular resort for Londoners, many of whom could only afford a day out at a time. Can you find the two towns on the map, and work out the distance between them? What other resorts were close enough to London for a day out? As you can see, the beach became very crowded in sunny weather. Can you see the camera with the notice offering photos at 6d a time? What can you tell about the way people dressed for the beach in the 1930s?

PAID HOLIDAYS

Towards the end of the 1930s a law was passed that employers should give their employees a minimum of one week's paid holiday a year. Until then, many workers could only take a holiday if they were prepared to miss their wages for a week, which was an impossible hardship for some of the poorer families. The Bill was discussed in Parliament on 27 November 1936:

Mrs Deering's father in the "beauty" competition at the Woolacombe holiday camp.

Mr Rowson: This Bill will make it obligatory on the part of employers to give to every employed person an annual holiday of eight consecutive days with pay. The present conditions are somewhat deplorable in certain trades and industries . . . practically 72 per cent of the working people [are] without an annual holiday with pay. In thousands of cases, especially in homes where there are three or four little children, it is not a question of providing for a holiday at the seaside, because even if holidays with pay were granted, they are in such straightened circumstances that they could not get away to the seaside for a day. . . . Psychologically, it would have a great effect on the employee to know that he would get a holiday which would help him to recuperate from the strain and stress of modern industry . . . even if he could only walk in the country.
(Hansard Parliamentary Proceedings)

43

Difficult Words

amateur	describes an activity done for a hobby, rather than for money.
anti-Semitism	being against people of Jewish birth.
annihilate	to do away with.
aquatic	to do with water.
back-to-back	describes houses which were built so that their back walls joined on to one another.
curriculum	plan of lessons and subjects taught in school.
"dolly"	This looked rather like a little wooden three-legged stool with a long handle. You took hold of the handle and thumped the "stool" up and down on the washing to get it clean.
espionage	spying.
fascism	a political creed which originated in Italy in the 1920s. In Britain fascist beliefs in the 1930s were strongly pro-British, anti-Communist and anti-Jewish. Fascists tended to react harshly and violently against anyone who did not share their views.
flora	flowers.
flunkey	footman.
hundredweight	112 lbs in weight.
imperative	necessary.
irrevocable	impossible to change.
lime-washed	an older form of white-washing, used to decorate walls or floors and to kill off any bugs lurking there.
motley	mixed.
peevish	ill-humoured, complaining.
poesy	poetry.
proscenium	front of stage or cinema screen.
quoits	a game played with rings, often made of rubber.
regiment	a group of soldiers in an army.
serge	a hard-wearing woollen cloth.
statistical analysis	working out facts and figures; in this case, to show how the company business was progressing.
sterilization	boiling or heating to destroy germs.
truncheon	a rounded stick carried by policemen.
verminous	infested with lice or other pests.
vim	a popular word of the times, meaning energy, vitality.
worsted	a kind of woollen material.

CONVERSION TABLE

NEW MONEY		OLD MONEY
1p	=	2.4d
5p	=	1s. (1 shilling)
50p	=	10s. (10 shillings)
£1	=	£1
		12d=1 shilling
		20 shillings=£1
£1.05	=	21 shillings (a guinea)

WAGES AND PRICES

Here are a few examples which may help you compare costs of the 1930s with those of today when you are working through this book:

National average wage	£4.00 per week
Rent of family house	from 7s per week to about £1 6s per week
New house	average £700 – £1,025
Loaf of bread	3d
Fuel bill for family for a week	approx 4s or more
1 lb cheese	10d
4 oz sweets	4d
Three-piece suite of furniture	£11
Visit to cinema	from 6d

=*Biographical Notes*=

People who have helped by recalling their memories for this book.

DEERING, Michael and Norma grew up in the 1930s. Today they run a village post office in Devon; Michael also works as a professional photographer, and Norma as a dressmaker. Michael was brought up in Hertfordshire and went to Merchant Taylor's School. He served in the armed forces in the war, and then spent many years in the electrical engineering industry. Norma's family lived in different locations in the Home Counties during her childhood. Her father worked in the Admiralty Department of the Civil Service. Later she took a degree at Reading University, and worked as a teacher until she had her four children.

LEADBEATER, Noel (b. 1920) was brought up in a large and poor family in Birmingham. She had to leave school at 14 and go out to work so that she could help the family's income. Later, after she married and had children, she worked in schools for mentally handicapped children, and was finally able to complete her studies by taking an Open University degree. She enjoys writing, and lives in Dorset with her husband, who is retired.

OAKES, Arthur (b. 1908) and Enid were farming in Warwickshire during the 1930s. Arthur learnt the skills of farming and of horse management from his father, and remembers the family's pet ponies being forcibly taken away for army use in the First World War. Arthur has studied all the scientific advances that have taken place in farming since the 1930s, but is now convinced that an organic, non-chemical approach to raising crops and livestock is the best. He keeps a herd of Jacob's sheep on his farm in Somerset. Enid runs a craft shop in the local village.

OWEN, Betty (b. 1914) spent part of the 1930s in Bournemouth. She took part in many local activities, such as choral societies and drama groups. She was also keen on cycling, and remembers a happy holiday spent touring the New Forest area by bike, staying at bed-and-breakfast places overnight. Later she worked as a nurse. Her husband worked in a bank, but he is now retired and they live in a small town in Lincolnshire.

PHILLIPS, Kathleen (b. 1913) is the daughter of a Baptist minister. She lived in the village of Soham, Cambridgeshire, and went to school in Ely. During the 1930s she attended Homerton teacher training college in Cambridge. She became engaged to be married, and the ceremony was planned for the autumn of 1939; then war was declared and all the elaborate preparations for church service, reception and honeymoon had to be abandoned, and the wedding was a quick and quiet one instead. She worked for many years as a teacher, and now lives in Shropshire.

Some authors quoted in the book.

FORRESTER, Helen was born into a wealthy family, and spent her early childhood in a comfortable home. However, her father's finances were ruined in the economic depression of the 1920s and '30s, and the family (with seven children) moved to Liverpool and rented a small house in a poverty-stricken area. Her family found it very hard to do without the luxuries to which they had been used, and her mother often preferred to try to scrape enough money to furnish one room well rather than to buy enough food for the children to eat. Helen slept on a wooden door covered in newspapers. She was expected to stay at home to look after her younger brothers and sisters, but eventually she managed to find a job in an office and was able to continue her education at evening classes. She suffered a lot of illness due to a poor diet and the hardships of living in slum conditions.

MITFORD, Jessica comes from a well-known family, who lived in Oxfordshire. One sister, Nancy, became a famous writer, another, Deboragh, is now the Duchess of Devonshire. The children were brought up to take their place in fashionable society, but Jessica finally rebelled against this and ran away abroad with her cousin, whom she later married. She joined the Communist Party and emigrated to America.

ORWELL, George was born in India in 1903, but moved back to England with his family in 1907. After being educated at Eton, he served in the Indian Imperial Police in Burma for several years and then returned to England to work as a teacher, and later as a literary editor. He became very interested in the conditions of people living in poor and difficult conditions, and set out to see for himself what it was like to be unemployed or homeless. He wrote up his experiences in *The Road to Wigan Pier* and *Down and Out in Paris and London.* He is also well-known for his novels *Animal Farm* and *Nineteen Eighty-Four,* in which his intentions are to show up some of the threatening aspects of modern society. Orwell's health was never good, and he suffered from tuberculosis; he died in 1950 at the age of 46.

SHARMAN, Nancy was born in 1925 and grew up in Southampton. Her father worked as a stevedore in the dockyards, arranging for cargoes to be loaded and unloaded. He drank a great deal and did not treat her mother well. He died when Nancy was seven. The family was left very poor, but fortunately, they had several relatives in the district who helped and supported them. They found plenty to enjoy with street games, visits to the cinema on Saturday mornings, picnics on the beach, and a trip to the fair when it came to the local common. If the children did not have any money, they would try to earn a few pennies by collecting rags and jam jars to sell to the rag-and-bone man. Her first job after leaving school was as a living-in servant; she had to start work at 5.30am and was paid only 6s a week.

Book List

Alan Delgado, *Have You Forgotten Yet?* (David and Charles, 1973)

Jane Dorner, *Fashion in the 20s and 30s* (Ian Allen, 1973)

S.E. Ellacott, *A History of Everyday Things in England, Volume V (1914-1968)* (Batsford, 1968)

Janet Flanner, *London was Yesterday, 1934-1939* (Michael Joseph, 1975)

James McMillan, *The Way It Happened* (William Kimber, 1980)

Graham Norton, *London before the Blitz* (Macdonald, 1970)

L.C.B. Seaman, *Life in Britain Between the Wars* (Batsford, 1970)

Frances Wilkins, *Growing up Between the Wars* (Batsford, 1979)

For older readers

Rene Cutforth, *Later Than We Thought* (David and Charles, 1976)

Jessica Mitford, *Hons and Rebels* (Victor Gollancz, 1961)

George Orwell, *The Road to Wigan Pier* (Victor Gollancz, 1937)

J.B. Priestley, *English Journey* (Heinemann, 1934)

Nancy Sharman, *Nothing to Steal* (Kaye and Ward, 1977)

SCOTLAND

NORTH SEA

0 ——— 100
Kms

Edinburgh

North Shields
Dunston

NORTHERN
IRELAND

IRISH SEA

Blackpool

Dublin

Wigan
Liverpool

Lincoln

Nottingham

Birmingham
Coventry

Harleston

Cambridge

WALES

ENGLAND

Merthyr Tydfil

Cardiff

London
Bromley
Croydon

Burnham-on-Sea
Glastonbury
Bridgwater

Lingfield

Southampton

Oakford

Gillingham
Rochester

Okehampton

Woolacombe

ENGLISH CHANNEL

47

Index